Honest, Kind and Friendly

A Lucky Duck Book

Promoting Children's Resilience and Wellbeing

Learning to be

Honest, Kind and Friendly

Karen Brunskill

P·C·P
Paul Chapman
Publishing

Paul Chapman Publishing
A SAGE Publications Company
1 Oliver's Yard
55 City Road
London EC1Y 1SP

SAGE Publications Inc.
2455 Teller Road
Thousand Oaks, California 91320

SAGE Publications India Pvt Ltd.
B-42, Panchsheel Enclave
Post Box 4109
New Delhi 110 017

www.luckyduck.co.uk

Commissioning Editor: George Robinson
Editorial Team: Mel Maines, Sarah Lynch, Wendy Ogden
Designer: Nick Shearn
Illustrations: Carlie Jennings, Jade, Ian Moule, Kelly Morris, Tony Wynn, Luke McFarlane, Hilda Knight, Lori Head

A catalogue record for this book is available from the British Library
Library of Congress Control Number 2006900195

ISBN13 978-1-4129-1962-3
ISBN10 1-4129-1962-2 (pbk)

Printed on paper from sustainable resources
Printed in Great Britain by The Cromwell Press Ltd, Trowbridge, Wiltshire

The CD-ROM contains PDF files, labelled 'Worksheets.pdf' which consists of the stories and worksheets for each unit in this resource. You will need Acrobat Reader version 3 or higher to view and print these resources.

The documents are set up to print to A4 but you can enlarge them to A3 by increasing the output percentage at the point of printing using the page set-up settings for your printer.

Contents

The *Promoting Children's Resilience and Wellbeing* series were originally published in Australia as the *Values for Life* series of books, and when we saw them we felt they would provide valuable additions to our range of books on emotional literacy. One of the attractions was that the four books provided a coherent programme from early years through to 12.

Book 1: *Learning to be Honest, Kind and Friendly* (Age range: 5 to 7)

Book 2: *Learning to be Confident, Determined and Caring* (Age range: 5 to 7)

Book 3: *Developing Consideration, Respect and Tolerance* (Age range: 7 to 9)

Book 4: *Enhancing Courage, Respect and Assertiveness* (Age range: 9 to 12)

In Australia the term 'emotional resilience' is more widely used than in the UK, though the term is increasingly current here. Resilience is the ability to recover from adversity or difficult situations or circumstances. Fuller (2001) suggests that life events are 'contagious'. Life events, both positive and negative, establish chains of behaviour. If children are faced with negative events their interpretation of these events will influence how they cope. If they don't have resilience they are likely to react in a negative way.

An example of a negative or risk chain would be:

> a child who grows up in violent circumstances and learns to distrust others, enters school and interprets the intention of others as hostile. The child then acts warily or aggressively towards peers and develops peer relationship problems…

An example of a positive or protective chain would be:

> a child who grows up in violent circumstances but learns, on entry to school, that there is a trustworthy adult who can be relied on to assist in the resolution of peer relationship difficulties. The child's positive attempts to interact with others are acknowledged. The child begins to feel accepted, mixes more appropriately with peers and develops a diversity of friendships. (Fuller, 2001)

The work of Goleman (1995) indicates that the promotion of protective factors in school life is not only predictive of academic success but even more importantly for positive adult life outcomes.

The idea of positive factors that promote resilience has been supported by research (Resnick, Harris and Blum, 1993; Fuller, McGraw and Goodyear, 1998). The main factors appear to be:

▸ family connectedness

▸ peer connectedness

▸ fitting in at school.

Two of these can be directly influenced by school life, creating positive experiences that are 'contagious'.

Resilience seems to depend largely on this sense of belonging. Once one belongs, empathy can develop and empathy builds group cohesion where moral actions such as honesty, altruism and caring emerge developmentally as the child matures.

This idea of resilience can be seen to be important in all areas of school life, as quoted in Fuller (2001):

> When schools promote belonging and ensure high levels of involvement between staff and students, bullying is reduced. (Citing the work of Olweus, 1995; Rigby 1996.)

This series, with its progressive programme, allows the opportunity for young people to explore:

▸ consideration	▸ courage	▸ tolerance
▸ honesty	▸ caring	▸ respect
▸ responsibility	▸ friendliness	▸ determination
▸ confidence	▸ kindness	▸ assertiveness.

As children mature the level that these can be explored becomes deeper; their reasoning and morality becomes more sophisticated with age and this type of programme can assist in their 'connectedness'. Our increasing awareness of the concept of 'Citizenship' should recognise elements such as empathy, moral reasoning and moral behaviour.

Current UK initiatives

The Healthy Schools Programme identifies emotional health and wellbeing (including bullying) as one of the areas schools have to develop and are required to produce evidence that they have met the necessary criteria. The Healthy Schools Programme, of course, is not a separate entity divorced from all other aspects of school development. The statutory components of PSHE and Citizenship for primary schools can be linked to the concept of emotional health and wellbeing and, we would also argue, emotional resilience.

The 12 domains covered in this programme fit the four components of PSHE and Citizenship at Key Stage 1 and 2:

1. Developing confidence and responsibility and making the most of their abilities.

2. Preparing to play an active role as citizens.

3. Developing a healthy, safer lifestyle.

4. Developing good relationships and respecting the difference between people.

The introduction of developing children's social, emotional and behavioural skills (SEBS) also highlights the importance of the type of material presented in this book.

▸ Emotional and social competence have been shown to be more influential than cognitive abilities for personal, career and scholastic success.

▸ Programmes that teach social and emotional competences have been shown to result in a wide range of educational gains.

▸ Work and workplace increasingly focus on social and emotional competences with increased emphasis on teamwork, communication, management skills etc. (DfES, 2003)

Though resilience is not mentioned directly, SEBS clearly identifies the earlier point about the 'contagious' effects of life events.

Research is bringing home the wide extent of various types of neglect and abuse. This is being exacerbated by the breakdown of extended family and communities which reduces support for the nuclear family, and the higher rates of divorce and subsequent one-parent families. This has led to a shake-up in belief that we can leave children's emotional and social development to parents... so schools have to provide the emotional and social guidance that some pupils currently lack. (DfES, 2003)

However, helping young people develop emotional resilience isn't just for young people from disturbed or disturbing backgrounds. School life and home life can be stressful for all young people, and with the growing awareness of the importance of emotional literacy, the *Promoting Children's Resilience and Wellbeing* series will be an ideal programme to support a key element, emotional resilience.

George Robinson and Barbara Maines

The *Promoting Children's Resilience and Wellbeing* series is a whole-school, values based programme. It is designed to assist in the creation of wellbeing and resilience in young students by introducing them to a range of values and behaviours that, when practised, can promote social and emotional health.

The programme, stories and activities are also designed to enhance the development of a positive learning environment and literacy skills.

Learning to be Honest, Kind and Friendly is suitable for 5 to 7 year olds. Each story introduces young students to the language and associated behaviours of six important values relevant to the development of social and emotional health of children in school settings:

1.   Consideration

2.   Friendliness

3.   Honesty

4.   Kindness

5.   Responsibility

6.   Tolerance.

Teacher's Notes

This series is designed to assist in the development of wellbeing and resilience in young students.

The values in the stories complement the following four areas:

1.   Social, emotional and behavioural skills

2.   Creation of supportive learning environments

3.   Development of language acquisition

4.   Development of wellbeing and resilience in young students.

Social, Emotional and Behavioural Skills

These stories introduce students, in a formal way, to the 'language' of prosocial values and behaviours that assist in promoting social and emotional wellbeing. Each story focuses upon identifiable values and behaviours that fit the requirements of the PSHE and Citizenship curriculum for children aged 5 to 12.

Creating Supportive Learning Environments

Students are more willing to participate in learning environments if they feel safe and secure in the classroom and have a sense of connectedness or bonding with their teachers and peers. A secure and supportive learning environment optimises the students' willingness to take risks.

The *Promoting Children's Resilience and Wellbeing* programme introduces students to the values and behaviours that assist in promoting a sense of safety, security, and social and emotional wellbeing in school settings. When practised, these values reinforce the development of three essential elements in the construction and maintenance of effective teaching and learning environments:

1.   A sense of safety and security.

2.   A sense of belonging.

3.   A sense of cooperation and harmony.

Development of Language Acquisition

The stories in the *Promoting Children's Resilience and Wellbeing* programme introduce young students to the 'language' of prosocial values and behaviours. The stories are designed to expand knowledge and understanding of many of the values and behaviours that assist in developing wellbeing, and to build language skills via listening, reading, discussion and related activities.

Development of Wellbeing and Resilience

The *Promoting Children's Resilience and Wellbeing* programme assists students in creating a better understanding of some of the related values and behaviours that help to promote social and emotional wellbeing and resilience. (See the chart on pages 3 and 4 for links.)

The stories are designed to support the development of resilience, focusing on three key areas:

1. **Self-appreciation**
   Introducing concepts of self-worth, self-efficacy, problem-solving skills, responsibility, courage to try new things, patience, acknowledging past successes and excellence.

2. **Social competence**
   Introducing concepts of friendliness, helpfulness, caring, empathy, flexibility, sense of humour, assertiveness, generosity, tolerance, courtesy, respect, fairness, cleanliness, cooperation, honesty, reliability, stress and anxiety management skills and forgiveness.

3. **Sense of optimistic future**
   Introducing concepts such as the importance of having goals, positive expectations, enthusiasm, determination, perseverance, self-discipline, optimism and organisational skills.

Guidelines for Value, Story and Resilience Links

These illustrate the links between the curriculum, value, story, resilience and wellbeing promoting factors.

VALUE	TITLE	SELF-APPRECIATION	SOCIAL COMPETENCE	SENSE OF OPTIMISTIC FUTURE	LINKS BETWEEN STORY, WELLBEING AND RESILIENCE
CONSIDERATION	Waking up Early		●	●	Recognising the need to consider other people when living in a group or family situation.
CONSIDERATION	Grandpa's Ankle	●	●		Demonstrating an ability to consider other people's needs if they are sick or disabled.
CONSIDERATION	Mrs King's Headache		●	●	Demonstrating the ability to show consideration in a classroom situation.
CONSIDERATION	My Brother Alan	●	●	●	Recognising the need to be extra considerate to family members during stressful times.
FRIENDLINESS	The Friendly Face	●	●		Recognising the importance of facial expressions and their implications in social settings. Identifying helpful gestures that encourage the making of friends.
FRIENDLINESS	A Friendly Smile	●	●		Recognising the positive impact that smiling at others usually creates.
FRIENDLINESS	Being Friendly		●	●	Being able to identify friendly behaviours.
FRIENDLINESS	My New School	●		●	Identifying friendly behaviours. Demonstrating a willingness to participate in social interactions with others.
HONESTY	Let's Colour In	●	●		Appreciating your best efforts.being cooperative and honest in building relationships with others.
HONESTY	At The Supermarket	●	●	●	Taking responsibility for found money. Communicating effectively with another, and recognition of a job well done.
HONESTY	Look What I Found	●	●		Having a problem and creating a way to solve it honestly.
HONESTY	The Blue Vase		●	●	Working together cooperatively to solve a problem. Focusing on building positive family relationships.

Guidelines for Value, Story and Resilience Links

VALUE	TITLE	SELF-APPRECIATION	SOCIAL COMPETENCE	SENSE OF OPTIMISTIC FUTURE	LINKS BETWEEN STORY, WELLBEING AND RESILIENCE
KINDNESS	Kyle's Bag of Sweets	●	●	●	How sharing helps build positive relationships with others in the family.
KINDNESS	In My Family	●	●	●	Knowing what I can offer others (e.g. time, money, etc). Being cooperative and caring. Seeing how this can help others.
KINDNESS	I Love Lemon Pie	●	●		Being able to organise the making of the pie, and a willingness to share.
KINDNESS	The Lunchbox	●	●	●	Facing a problem of 'no lunch'. Recognising the friendliness and cooperation of others in preventing hunger later.
RESPONSIBILITY	A Day At The Beach	●	●	●	Recognising and demonstrating an ability to be personally responsible for own sun safety.
RESPONSIBILITY	My New Pony	●	●	●	Recognising the need to be a responsible pet owner and all that it entails.
RESPONSIBILITY	Sally's New School	●	●		Demonstrating good organisational skills and responsibility for personal belongings.
RESPONSIBILITY	Waiting For The Rain	●	●	●	Recognising and demonstrating an understanding of water conservation and how we can help a potentially difficult environmental situation by being responsible water users.
TOLERANCE	My Little Sister	●	●		Appreciating our differences. Demonstrating caring and a sense of humour. Tolerating younger sibling's behaviour.
TOLERANCE	My School Friends	●	●	●	Appreciating our differences and acknowledging the worth of others.
TOLERANCE	Grandpa's Music	●	●	●	Appreciating individual taste in music. Being polite, friendly and flexible. Maintaining positive relationships.
TOLERANCE	The Family Picnic	●	●	●	Recognition and appreciation of family differences. Maintaining positive relationships. Displaying tolerance and consideration for others.

To use the programme the facilitator will:

▶ Choose a prosocial value as a focus.

▶ Print or photocopy the relevant story for your students. Each story has two accompanying activity sheets.

▶ Read and discuss the story with the students identifying the specific prosocial values. This will assist students in building a language of prosocial values and behaviours.

▶ Ask the students to paste the story into a scrapbook. The scrapbook can be taken home and read with the family.

The Programme

1. Consideration

2. Friendliness

3. Honesty

4. Kindness

5. Responsibility

6. Tolerance

1

One Sunday, I woke up early.

2

Mum was asleep.

3

Dad was asleep.

4

My sister was asleep.

5

My brother was asleep.

6

The dog was asleep.

7

I played very quietly.

8

Everyone said I was very considerate.

Activity 1

Colour in the outlined words.

In the story, the girl woke up early and found that her:

Mum was asleep

Dad was asleep

Sister was asleep

Brother was asleep.

She played very quietly.

She was very

considerate.

Activity 2

Draw about a time you woke up early and showed consideration.

Fill in the missing letters.

She was very

_ _ _ _ _ _ _ _ _ _ _ _ _ _ _ _ _ _.

1

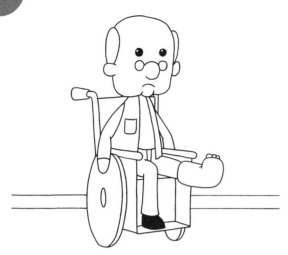

Grandpa broke his ankle.

2

I read a book to Grandpa.

3

I made a cup of tea for Grandpa.

4

I collected the mail for Grandpa.

5

I watered the plants for Grandpa.

6

I played chess with Grandpa.

7

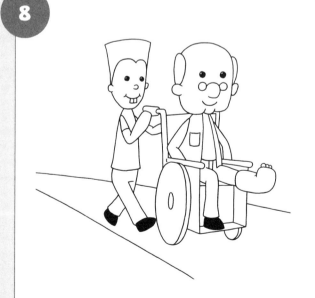

I made Grandpa Laugh.

8

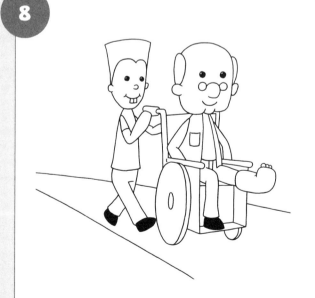

Grandpa said that I was very considerate.

Activity 1

In the story, Grandpa had a broken ankle.
The boy did many things for his grandpa.

Use the clues to fill in the missing words.

He read a _ _ _ _.

He made a _ _ _ of tea.

He collected the _ _ _ _.

He watered the _ _ _ _ _ _.

He played _ _ _ _ _.

He was very

_ _ _ _ _ _ _ _ _ _ _ _ _.

Consideration – Grandpa's Ankle

Activity 2

In the story, the grandchild did many things for his grandpa.

Colour in the sentence below.

Try to be considerate.

Rewrite the line above.

_ _ _ _ _ _ _ _

_ _ _ _ _ _ _ _ _ _ •

18

1

It was a hot day.

Mrs King had a bad headache.

2

She asked if we could be considerate and work very quietly.

We all agreed.

3

Some of us read books quietly.

4

Some of us worked quietly on our projects.

5

Some of us quietly played games.

6

Mrs King said we were all very considerate.

Activity 1

Answer Yes or No to the following questions.

If someone in your family had a headache, would you:

- Make lots of noise?   _____

- Play quietly?   _____

- Have a party?   _____

- Read quietly?   _____

- Be very considerate if
  you made lots of noise?   _____

Design a sign that lets others know that someone in the family has a headache and consideration is needed.

Activity 2

List some things that you could do if you were being considerate of someone else. List things that are very considerate and others that are not.

Very considerate	Not very considerate

1

My big brother Alan was studying to be a doctor.

2

He had to spend a lot of time reading and writing.

Sometimes he didn't have time to play.

3

So, when Alan was reading, I was reading too.

4

When Alan was writing, I was writing too.

5

Sometimes, Alan needed to work quietly in his room.

6

So, I worked quietly in my room too.

7

Alan said that I was very considerate, and that he would be able to play that afternoon.

8

We both had lots of fun playing.

Activity 1

Write down the ways that Alan's younger brother was considerate.

1. When Alan was reading, what did his younger brother do?

2. When Alan was writing, what did his younger brother do?

3. When Alan was in his room, what did his younger brother do?

4. How did the younger brother show that he was considerate of Alan's situation?

Activity 2

In the story, the brother was very

— — — — — — — — — — — — — — —•

Draw or write about how you would be considerate of a family member if they had something important to do.

Friendliness

1

This is a happy face.

2

This is a sad face.

3

This is a laughing face.

4

This is an angry face.

5

This is a sleepy face.

6

This is a surprised face.

7

This is a friendly face.

Activity 1

Colour in the outlined words.

This is a happy face.

This is a sad face.

This is an angry face.

This is a sleepy face.

This is a friendly face.

Activity 2

Draw faces in the boxes below.

A sad face

A happy face

An angry face

A friendly face

A sleepy face

1

I smiled at the postlady.

She smiled at me.

2

I smiled at the policeman.

He smiled at me.

3

I smiled at the shop owner.

She smiled at me.

4

I smiled at the traffic officer.

He smiled at me.

5

I smiled at Mum.

She smiled at me.

6

I smiled at my teacher.

He smiled at me.

7

I smiled at my friends.

They all smiled back at me.

Activity 1

Fill in the missing letters from the story.

In the story, the girl s_ _ _ _ _ at the postlady, _ _ _ _ _ _d at the policeman, s_ _ _ _d at the shop owner, _ _ _ _ _ _ _ at her mum and smiled at her _ _ _ _ _ _ _ _ _.

Activity 2

Draw a portrait of your family, all with friendly smiles.

My Family Portrait

1

My dog wags his tail when he's being friendly.

2

My cat purrs loudly when she's being friendly.

3

My horse rubs his face on me when he's being friendly.

4

My goldfish blows bubbles when it's being friendly.

5

My sister shares with me when she's being friendly.

6

My neighbour waves when he's being friendly.

7

And I smile a lot when I am being friendly.

Activity 1

Fill in the missing letters.

My _ _ _ wags his tail when he's being friendly.

My _ _ _ purrs loudly when she's being friendly.

My goldfish _ _ _ _ _ bubbles when it's being friendly.

I _ _ _ _ _ a lot when I'm being _ _ _ _ _ _ _ _ _.

Friendliness – Being Friendly

Activity 2

In each of the boxes, draw what the animal does when it is being friendly.

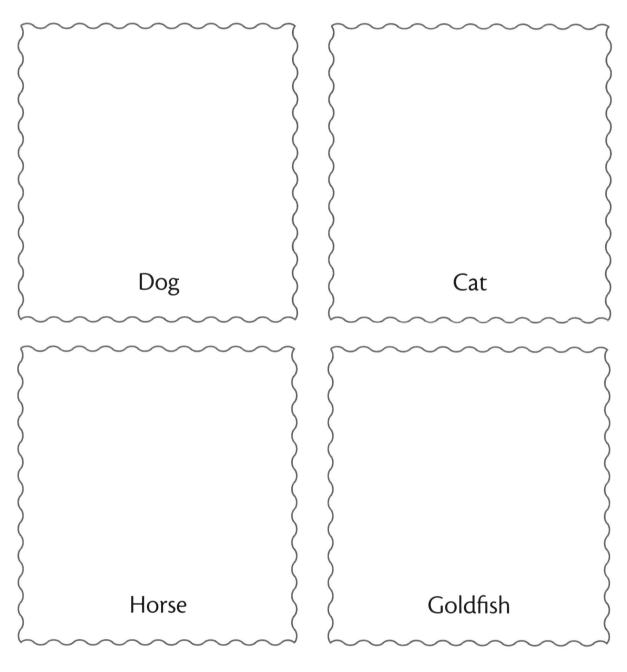

Dog

Cat

Horse

Goldfish

Look through a newspaper or magazine to find pictures of people being friendly, and paste them on to a large class poster.

1

It was my first day at a new school.

I hope it is friendly, I thought.

2

My teacher introduced me to the class.

They all looked very friendly.

3

At playtime, Gita and Sam asked me to play hide-and-seek with them.

That was friendly.

4

At lunch-time, Peter and Kelly shared some fruit with me.

That was friendly.

5

At home time, Gita, Sam, Peter and Kelly all walked with me to the gate.

That was friendly.

6

At my new school, the teacher and children were all very friendly.

Activity 1

Fill in the missing words from the story.

In the story, the girl was going to a new school.

The _ _ _ _ _ _ _ introduced her to the class.

Gita asked her to play _ _ _ _ and _ _ _ _.

Peter and Kelly shared some _ _ _ _ _ with her.

At _ _ _ _ _ _ _ _ Gita and all the children _ _ _ _ _ _ to the gate with her.

They were all very _ _ _ _ _ _ _ _ _.

Activity 2

Draw a picture of yourself at a new school and write about how you would make new friends.

1

I entered a colouring competition.

2

I put my name on the picture.

3

I put my age on the picture.

4

It is important to be honest about your age in competitions.

5

I coloured the best I could.

6

7

I won a prize.

Activity 1

The Colouring Competition

Colour the picture below and be honest about your age.

Name..

Age ....

Activity 2

Write down why it is important to be honest about your age in competitions.

In competitions you need to know your address too.

Write your address on the front of the envelope below.

1

I went to the supermarket with Mum. Mum took a long time at the checkout.

2

I asked Mum if I could have an ice cream. 'Sorry,' said Mum, 'but I don't have enough money today.'

3

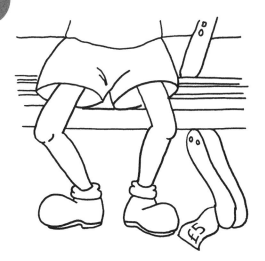

As I sat down on a seat to wait for Mum, I noticed a £5.00 note under my feet.

4

I picked it up. I was about to put the money into my pocket when I saw an old lady sitting nearby.

5

She was looking for something inside her bag. 'Excuse me, did you drop some money?' I asked.

6

'Yes, I had a £5.00 note. I need it to catch the bus home,' she said.

I handed her the money.

7

'I think this belongs to you,' I said. 'Thank you very much,' said the old lady.

8

I walked back to Mum and told her what I had done.

9

As we left the supermarket, the old lady came up to us.

She had bought an ice cream in a cone.

10

The old lady handed me the ice cream and said,

'Thank you for your honesty.'

11

'Thank you for the ice cream,' I said with a big smile.

Activity 1

Fill in the missing word in the sentence below.

In the story, the old lady handed the boy an ice cream for his

_ _ _ _ _ _ _ _ .

Colour in your favourite flavoured ice cream cone.

Chocolate

Raspberry Ripple

Peppermint

Strawberry

Vanilla

Activity 2

The boy in the story practised honesty.

Write and draw about a time when you were honest.

1

'Mum, look what I've found – a box with an old ring inside.

It must belong to someone.'

'Let's see if we can find the owner,' said Mum.

2

We knocked on Mr Smith's door. Knock knock!

'Does this belong to you?' we asked.

'No, that does not belong to me,' said Mr Smith.

3

We spoke to Mr Jones in his garden.

'Does this belong to you?' we asked.

'No, that does not belong to me,' said Mr Jones.

4

We knocked on Mr Kelly's door. Knock knock!

'Does this belong to you?' we asked.

'Oh yes! I've been looking everywhere for that,' said Mr Kelly.

5

'It has a ring inside it that used to belong to my father. It is very special to me,' said Mr Kelly.

6

'Thank you both very much for your honesty,' said Mr Kelly.

Activity 1

The boy in the story found a beautiful ring. Colour the rings below and match the shape of the ring to the correct word.

Red stone **Circle**

Blue stone **Rectangle**

Green stone **Diamond**

Orange stone **Square**

Add the rings together.

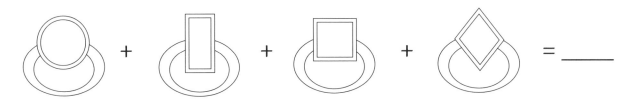

On the back of the sheet, draw a ring that you would like to wear.

Activity 2

Help the boy find his way to the ring.

Draw your own maze with a special ring at the end.

Try out your maze with a friend.

1

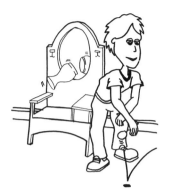

One rainy day, my sisters and I were playing inside.

We bumped the hall stand and Mum's favourite blue vase crashed to the floor.

2

Mum heard the loud crash and came running into the room. She looked angry.

3

'Who broke my vase?' asked Mum. 'Not me,' said Tony.

4

'Who broke my vase?' asked Mum. 'Not me,' said Jenny.

5

'Who broke my vase?' asked Mum. 'Not me,' said Millie.

6

'Someone broke the vase,' said Mum. She looked at all of us.

7

'We are sorry, Mum,' we all said. 'It was an accident.'

'Thank you for being honest,' said Mum.

8

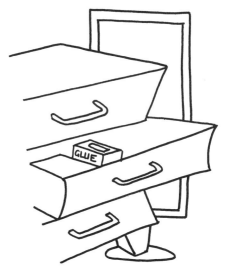

'Can you all help me find the glue?' asked Mum.

Activity 1

Colour in the outlined words.

In the story, Mum asks,

'Who broke my vase?'

Draw what you think Mum's face might have looked like when she was asking that question?

> **Angry?**
>
> **Happy?**
>
> **Sad?**
>
> **Excited?**

On the back of this sheet, write about a time when you were honest about something.

Activity 2

Colour the broken pieces of the vase blue. Cut the pieces out and paste the vase back together.

1

Kyle went to a birthday party.

2

He came home with a bag of mixed sweets.

3

Kyle gave one to his big sister. 'Thank you for being so kind,' she said.

4

Kyle gave one to his little sister. 'Thank you for being so kind,' she said.

5

Kyle gave one to his mum.

'Thank you for being so kind,' said Mum.

6

Kyle gave one to his dad.

Thank you for being so kind,' said Dad.

7

Kyle ate all the other sweets.
Yum!

Activity 1

Cut out all the sweets below and give two to each member of the family.

Activity 2

Colour in the outlined word then fill in the missing word.

Kyle was very

when he shared his sweets.

It was very _ _ _ _

of him to share.

On the back of this sheet, draw or write about a time you shared with your family.

1

In my family, we like to be kind in lots of ways.

2

Sometimes, Mum delivers meals to people.

3

Sometimes, Dad helps at my school.

4

Sometimes, my sister makes cakes for her club.

5

Sometimes, Nana helps in the charity shop.

6

Sometimes, I put money into a tin.

7

And sometimes, my dog likes to help in the garden.

Whoops!

Activity 1

Draw lines to match the sentence with the correct picture, then colour in.

Mum delivers meals to people.

Dad helps at my school.

My sister makes cakes for her club.

Nana helps in the charity shop.

I put money in a tin.

On the back of this sheet, write about how you are kind.

Draw a picture of you being kind.

Activity 2

I put money in a tin to help other people.

How much money did I put in the tin?

(10p) + (10p) + (10p) = _____

(5p) + (10p) + (10p) = _____

(20p) + (10p) + (10p) = _____

Mum delivered 10 meals. Fill in the missing number.

4 meals + _____ meals = 10 meals

2 meals + _____ meals = 10 meals

7 meals + _____ meals = 10 meals

_____ meals + 5 meals = 10 meals

1

On Saturday, I asked Mum if she could make a lemon pie. 'Yes,' said Mum.

2

'But we need some lemons,' she said. I was so excited, I found my bucket and ran next door.

3

I asked Mrs Smith if I could pick some lemons from her tree.

'Sure,' she said.

4

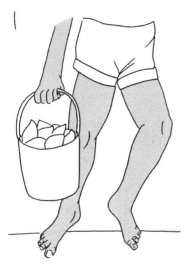

I filled my bucket with lemons and then I walked home. On the way, I met...

5

the postman. I gave him some lemons. 'Thank you, that is very kind,' he said.

6

I saw Mr Wong in his garden. I gave him some lemons. 'Thank you, that is very kind,' he said.

7

I gave the other lemons to Mum. She used some of them to make the lemon pie.

8

When the pie was cooked, we cut a big slice and put it on a special plate. I carefully carried it to Mrs Smith's.

9

I knocked on the door. When Mrs Smith opened the door, she got such a surprise. 'I love lemon pie. Thank you. That is very kind of you,' she said.

'No, thank you for sharing your lemons,' I said.

Activity 1

Cut each pie into pieces.

Then finish the sentence with a word from below.

Cut the pie into two equal pieces.

I cut the pie in _____.

Cut the pie into three equal pieces.

I cut the pie into _____.

Cut the pie into four equal pieces.

I cut the pie into _____.

thirds   half   quarters

Draw a lemon pie on the back of the sheet.

Cut it into enough pieces for every member of your family to eat. How many pieces did you cut the pie into? _____

Activity 2

There were 20 lemons in the basket.

I gave 5 lemons to the postman.

Draw the lemons.

$$20 - \boxed{} = \underline{}$$

I gave 5 lemons to Mr Wong.

Draw the lemons.

$$15 - \boxed{} = \underline{}$$

I gave 7 lemons to Mum.

Draw the lemons.

$$10 - \boxed{} = \underline{}$$

Draw how many lemons were left in the basket.

1

One day, I left my lunchbox at home.

At lunch-time, I was very sad and very hungry too.

2

I told my teacher. She told the class. Soon, some of my friends were sharing their lunches with me.

3

Raphael gave me some salami and cheese.

4

Jai gave me some celery sticks and dip.

5

Kim gave me half a jam sandwich.

6

Samantha gave me a cake and some cherries.

7

My friends were very kind to share their food. I felt very happy and I had a very full tummy.

8

I hope I remember my lunchbox tomorrow...

or do I?

Activity 1

Colour in the outlined sentence below.

My friends were very
kind when they shared
their food with me.

Find the answers to these sums.

3 + 🍒 = _____ cherries

🥬 + 5 = _____ celery sticks

🍰🍰 + 4 = _____ cakes

🍎🍎 + 6 = _____ apples

Activity 2

Join the dots from 1 to 40, then colour in.

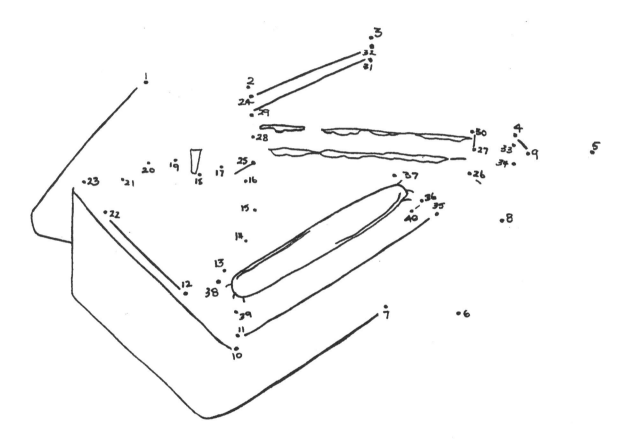

Draw some healthy food for your lunchbox.

1

'Let's go for a day at the beach,' said Mum.

'Yes please,' I cheered.

'You will need to take responsibility for yourself, and make sure that you are protected from the hot sun,' said Mum.

2

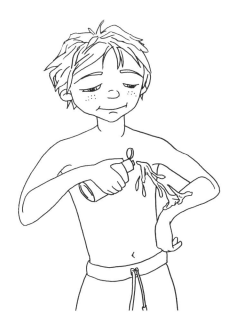

I put on my sunscreen.

3

I put on my hat.

4

I put on my sunglasses.

5

I put on my shirt.

6

I am ready for my day at the beach!

Activity 1

Colour in the outlined words.

In the story, the boy put on:

sunscreen,

sunglasses,

a hat and a

shirt.

He was very

responsible.

Activity 2

Below are all the things you need to take to the beach if you are being responsible.

Draw each of the items in their boxes.

sunglasses

hat

sunscreen

shirt

1

I have a lovely new pony.

I am responsible for her.

2

Every day, I make sure my pony has water.

3

Every day, I make sure my pony is safe.

4

Every day, I make sure my pony is brushed.

5

Every day, I make sure my pony has food.

6

Mum says I am a responsible pet owner.

7

I love my pony, and I think she loves me too.

Activity 1

Draw the correct items in each box.

In the story, the girl is responsible for her pony. Draw pictures in each box showing you being responsible for your pet.

Giving your pet water

Feeding your pet

Brushing or washing your pet

Keeping your pet safe

Activity 2

Answer the following questions with Yes or No.

Do you have a pet? _____

Does your pet have a name? _____

Do you make sure your pet is safe? _____

Do you make sure your pet is looked after?

_____

Do you make sure your pet has lots of water?

_____

Do you make sure your pet has food? _____

Every day, do you make sure your pet is not

lonely? _____

1

Sally was starting at a new school.

Sally's Mum said that putting her name on her belongings was a responsible thing to do.

Sally put her name on her books.

2

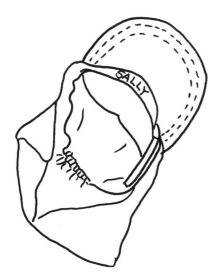

Sally put her name on her hat.

3

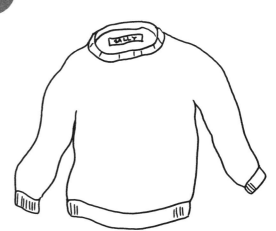

Sally put her name on her jumper.

4

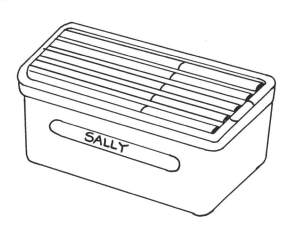

Sally put her name on her lunchbox.

5

Sally put her name on her pencils.

6

Sally put her name on her bag.

7

Sally's name was now on all of her belongings and she was ready for school.

Activity 1

Sally was responsible when she started school.

Draw the items that you would name when starting at a new school. Don't forget to label them!

Fill in the missing letters.

Mum said it was a very

_ _ _ _ _ _ _ _ _ _ _ _

thing to do.

Activity 2

Colour in these outlined words from the story:

Jumper

Bag

Hat

Pencils

Books

Lunchbox

1

We live on a farm. Sometimes, it doesn't rain very much.

2

Our water comes from water tanks.

3

We make sure we turn off dripping taps.

4

We reuse any waste water on the gardens.

5

We plant trees that do not need much water.

6

We make sure we have quick showers.

7

We have to be responsible with water.

8

When it rains, we dance and sing.

Activity 1

Using the pictures as clues, answer the following questions.

In the story, where is water stored?

What type of showers do they have?

What do they do with dripping taps?

What sort of plants do they grow?

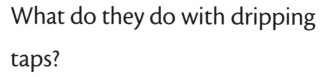

What do they have to be with water?

What do they do when it rains?

Activity 2

List some things that you know save water, and some things that do not save water.

Being responsible with water	Being irresponsible with water

1

My little sister is fun to play with. But I need to be tolerant with her because she can be very messy!

Sometimes, I can even tell where she has been.

Oh no, my little sister has been here. She has opened the crisps.

2

Oh no, my little sister has been here. She has opened the drawers.

3

Oh no, my little sister has been here. She has unrolled the toilet paper.

4

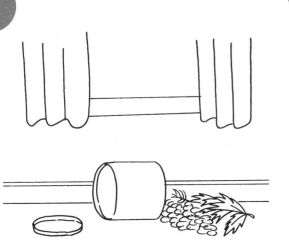

Oh no, my little sister has been here. She has pushed the plant over.

5

Oh no, my little sister has been here. She has put on Mum's make-up.

6

Shhh, my little sister is asleep!

Please don't wake her up.

Activity 1

Cut out the pictures below and match them to the correct sentences.

My little sister has opened the crisps.

My little sister has put on Mum's make-up.

My little sister has pushed the plant over.

My little sister has unrolled the toilet paper.

Activity 2

Colour in the outlined word.

I need to be tolerant with my little sister.

Draw your favourite part of the story in the space below.

1

My friends at school all like to do different things.

Tolerance is accepting different things in people.

2

There is Ravi who is very tall and loves to play sport.

3

There is Susie who wears bright clothes and dances to strange music.

4

There is Anna who has long hair and likes to play the drums loudly.

5

And there is Jane who has lovely eyes and likes to paint large, colourful pictures.

6

I think it is good that my friends are all different.

Activity 1

My friends are all different.

Draw a friend who is tall.

Draw a friend who likes sport.

Draw a friend who likes to paint.

Draw a friend who likes music.

Activity 2

Colour in the outlined word.

Tolerance is accepting people's differences.

Write or draw how you are different from some of your friends.

Write or draw how you are the same as some of your friends.

1

My grandpa lives near the beach. I like to visit him, except when he plays his music.

2

Mum says I need to be more tolerant of Grandpa's music, and she says, 'It is good that we all like different sorts of music.'

3

Grandpa is in a folk band. He plays the violin and the mouth organ. Sometimes, he sings.

4

When we visit him, he is always playing music. When we eat, he plays the violin.

5

When we talk, he plays the mouth organ. Sometimes, at parties, he plays them both.

6

If we ask him to stop playing his music, he starts to sing.

7

I like to go to Grandpa's to visit, except when he plays his music.

Activity 1

Fill in the missing word.

Mum said that I need to be more _ _ _ _ _ _ _ _ _ of Grandpa's music.

Draw lines to connect all the words to the instruments.

Violin
Trumpet
Tambourine
Drums
Guitar
Mouth organ

Draw your favourite instrument on the back of the sheet.

Activity 2

Add up the instruments.

 + 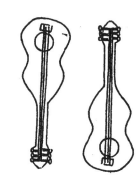 = _____

 +   = _____

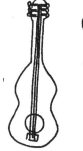 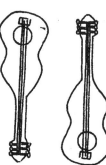 + = _____

How many instruments altogether? _____

1

One Sunday every year, we have a family picnic.

All my aunties, uncles and cousins come along.

2

Aunty Joy makes cakes and loves singing.

She wants everyone to join in a sing-along after lunch.

3

Aunty May is going deaf.

Sometimes, I need to yell so that she hears me.

4

My little cousin, Alex, is a very messy eater.

5

Old Uncle Les has bad eyesight, but always plays cricket.

We let him have lots of chances before he goes out.

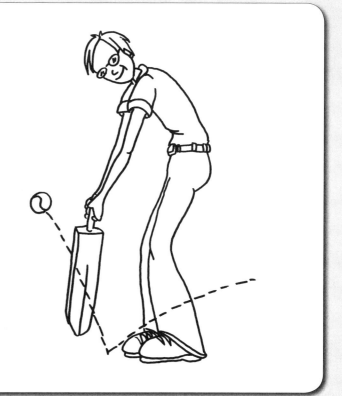

6

Uncle Bill takes his false teeth out after lunch.

He puts them in his pocket so he won't lose them. Yuk!

7

And there is Nana, who gives us lots and lots of sloppy kisses.

Sometimes, I have to be very tolerant.

8

But that's what families are about.

Activity 1

Draw lines to match each sentence to the correct picture, then colour in.

Uncle Bill takes out his false teeth.

Nana gives me lots of sloppy kisses.

Uncle Les has bad eyesight but always plays cricket.

My cousin, Alex, is a messy eater.

Aunty Joy makes cakes and loves to sing.

On the back of the sheet, write three interesting things about your family.

Activity 2

Below is an empty picnic basket.

Draw six different items that you would like to take on a family picnic.

Label each one, then colour in.

Benard, B. (1995) *Fostering Resiliency in Kids: Protective Factors in the Family, School and Community*, Western Centre for Drug Free Schools and Communities, Portland, Oregon.

Cahill, H. (1999) Why a Whole-school Approach to Enhancing Resilience?, *Mindmatters Newsletter*, March, p 2.

Canfield, J. and Siccone, F. (1995) *101 Ways to Develop Student Self-esteem and Responsibility*, Massachussetts, Allyn and Bacon.

Cantor, R., Kivel, P. and Creighton, A. (1997) *Days of Respect: Organising a School-wide Violence Prevention Programme*, Hunter House, California.

Catalano, R. and Hawkins, J.D. (Ed) 'The social development model: a theory of antisocial behaviour'. In Hawkins J.D. (Ed) *Delinquency and Crime: Current Theories*, New York, Cambridge Publications.

Centre for Adolescent Health (1998) *The Gatehouse Project: Promoting Emotional Wellbeing: A Whole-school Approach, Team Guidelines*, Centre for Adolescent Health, Melbourne.

Department of Education, Victoria (1999) *Framework for Student Services in Victorian Schools: Teacher resource*, Department of Education, Victoria.

DfES (2003) *Developing children's social, emotional and behavioural skills: a whole curriculum approach*. Primary National Strategy.

Fuller, A. (2001) Background Paper on Resilience presented to the Northern Territory Principal's Association (Australia).

Fuller, A., McGraw, K. and Goodyear, M. (1998) *The Mind of Youth*. Department of Education, Melbourne, Australia.

Fuller, A. (1998) *From Surviving to Thriving: Promoting Mental Health in Young People*, ACER Press, Melbourne.

Goleman, D. (1995) *Emotional Intelligence – Why it matters more than IQ*, London, Bloomsbury.

Hawkins, J. and Catalano, R. (1993) *Communities that Care: Risk and Protective Focused Prevention Using the Social Development Strategy*, Developmental Research and Programmes Incorporated, Seattle, USA.

Lickona, T. (1997) 'Educating for Character: a comprehensive approach' in Molnar (ed.) *The Construction of Children's Character*, University of Chicago Press, Chicago.

Olweus, D. (1995) Bullying or Peer Abuse at School – facts and interventions, *Current Directions in Psychological Science*, 4,6, p 196-200.

Resnick, M.D., Harris, L.J. and Blum, R.W. (1993) The impact of caring and connectedness on adolescent health and wellbeing, *Journal of Paediatrics and Child Health*, 29.

Rigby, K. (1996) *Bullying in schools and what we can do about it*, ACER Press, Melbourne, Australia.

Seligman, M. (1995) *The Optimistic Child*. NSW: Random House, Australia.

Smith, C. and McKee, S. (2005) *Becoming an Emotionally Healthy School*, A Lucky Duck Book, Paul Chapman, London.

Taylor, M. (2000) 'Values Education: Issues and challenges in policy and school practice' in M. Leicester, C. Modgil and S. Modgil (ed.), *Education, Culture and Values*, Vol 2, Falmer Press London.